Beautifully Valued

THINGS I WISH MY **dad** would have told me

Ava Blalark, LCSW

Published and distributed in the United States by Ava L. Blalark, LCSW. Inherently Valued, LLC. Chicago, Illinois

Copyright © 2022 by Ava L. Blalark, LCSW

All rights reserved. No parts of this book be reproduced by any mechanical, photographic, or electronic process, or in the form of phonographic recording; nor may it be stored in a retrieval system, transmitted, or otherwise be copied for public or private use – other than for "fair use" as brief quotations embodied in articles and reviews – without prior written permission of the publisher.

The author of this book does not dispense medical advice or prescribe any technique as a form of treatment for physical, emotional, or medical problems without a physician's advice, either directly or indirectly. The author intends to offer information of a general nature to help you in your quest for emotional and spiritual well-being. If you use any of the information in this book for yourself, which is your constitutional right, the author or publisher assume no responsibility for your actions.

Certain names and other identifying information have been changed to protect and honor the innocent and those whose innocence has been lost, stolen, taken or given away.

Cover Design – Okomota

Editing – Doris Foster

Interior Design – Istvan Szabo, Ifj

Proofreading – Doris Foster

Back Cover Photo Headshot - Chollette

ISBN 13: 978-1-7360071-2-9

Printed in the United States of America

www.avalblalark.com

ACKNOWLEDGMENTS

Here we are for round 2 and for some reason this one seemed both harder to write and easier at the same. Easier in the sense that I knew where I was going and where I wanted to end up. Harder in the sense that I realized some new things about myself and some of it was hard to face, but it all makes me who I am today and I like me.

Once again and forever, I want to thank God for taking everything evil supposedly meant for me and turning it around for my good. Thank you for helping me to see me as you see me. I am loved and valued. Beautifully valued.

For my husband and my son - The Korrons, my boys. I hope I make you proud. Thank you for your love and support.

To my parents who I'm forever grateful. Both for their love, their sacrifice, and their unfailing support in my life when I need it most.

To my siblings - Cinny, Mike, and Demi. You guys are what I need, you keep me on my toes and I am honored to be your big sister.

My grandparents - Grandparents are graced with a special something from God. Their unconditional love, support, patience, and everything else is other worldly. I've seen it with my grandparents and I've seen it with others. The world is a better place because of all of you.

To my Spiritual leaders - I was raised in the church and throughout my life, I have had so many people positively invest in me. While it may not appear that I am always paying attention I am always getting exactly what I need. Thank you for allowing God to lead you so that you may lead me. Pastor Matthew Pettis Jr. - My grandfather and first pastor, teacher, and leader. I may have been too young to understand it but I thank you for being the best grandpa a girl could ask for. Your quiet strength was everything. The way you cared for and gave to those around you is still inspiring to me.

Pastor Steven and Lora Pettis, obeyed and followed in his footsteps. Thank you for shaping my young adult life.

Pastor Walter H. Blalark my father in love and pastor. Thank you for your wisdom and your sacrifice to all of those around you. Thank you for being such an example of a Godly man.

Thank you, Robin Devonish, for making my dream a reality.

DEDICATION

This book is dedicated to my father whom I love dearly. We got off to the best start! You laid a solid foundation. The middle parts got a little tough…lol but because of that foundation, we always find our footing. I thank God for forgiveness, love, and restoration. Even at my big age, I can still be a "daddy's girl."

Love "the eldest" but also known as "little one"

For my grandfather whom I love fiercely. There's no one alive who could ever take your place. I never would have gotten this far without your love. I still think of you daily and I hope I make you proud. It's all I've ever wanted to do.

Love "Fugee"

My Uncle Chris (Uncle Stovie) - who has always been like a second dad. I will always remember you for your honesty and your humor, for the way you gave when you didn't have it to give. From you, I have learned that perfection is not the goal but life truly is a marathon.

Love "Grippy"

I pray that this book is not just me telling you some things about my life. You may or may not have had similar experiences. I hope that this book guides you or reminds you of the love of an everlasting and ever- present Father who is with you even in your darkest times.

CONTENTS

Introduction... 1

Chapter 1: *Hero*...5

Chapter 2: *What's in a name?*...13

Chapter 3: *Conflicted*..25

Chapter 4: *Beauty's only Skin deep* 34

Chapter 5: *The Blues of the Past*....................................40

Chapter 6: Into the Unknown..47

Chapter 7: *Rejection*..56

Chapter 8: *The Choice*...62

Chapter 9: *Father Figures*...69

Conclusion: *Restoration*...75

References...78

Introduction

In Valued: Things I wish my mom would have told me I introduced you to the concept of inherent value. These two words have stuck with me and have become my mantra. To me, it means that no matter what you go through, what you do, and regardless of how you feel or think about it you have value. That value was with you when you were born and it will stay with you until the day you die and maybe even in the afterlife. Sometimes the situations we go through in life cause us to feel unworthy, unloved, and dirty even when we find ourselves in predicaments through no fault of our own. You matter and if you never knew the point before now, remember that you are the point. What is the point in healing? You are. What is the point in talking about it? You are. What's the point of it all? You are. You are inherently valued...you are beautifully valued. I haven't always thought I was beautiful (inside or out). I suffered with my self-esteem regarding my appearance. I questioned who I was and if I mattered at all. I haven't always thought I was valuable, especially to anyone outside of myself. But God sends angels to remind me of just how loved I am and how important I am to Him and to others.

This book is meant to delve a little deeper into what it means to be beautifully valued. As I thought about this, I knew the focus this time around would be my father, my earthly father. I joked that he would have to get on the same chopping block as my mother. As I continued to explore my relationship with my father, I realized I could not talk about the inherent value or beautiful value without talking about my heavenly father. I did not just pull myself up by my own bootstraps. It was the strength of my parents even in their messiness, it was the strength of my grandparents stepping in, it was countless aunts, uncles, and cousins. Most importantly and undoubtedly, it was God. The realization of my inherent value and worth comes from above. Once I wrapped my head around the fact that I am truly the daughter of a King there was no stopping me. He cares about me. He cares about the things that concern me and he wants me to be whole- mentally, physically, spiritually, financially, relationally and any other "-ly" you can think of. Now that doesn't mean that life is perfect. If you read *Things I wish my mother would have told me*, then you know. It's up to you to go after all of your "lys". God has a plan for you. And just like there is a God, there is a devil who uses any means, even people to hurt you and situations to break you. And sometimes we make our own stupid choices that get us into situations that we don't know how to get out of. It doesn't matter because whatever is meant for bad, God can turn around for your good. You can still turn pain into purpose. God thought of you before you were even born. He put you together and made you wonderful because all of His work is

Beautifully Valued

---

wonderful. The sun, the moon, the stars, the oceans, and everything in between are all His work. We marvel at and still contemplate and study the wonders of this universe. You too are a work of God, as precious and as unique as every star in the sky. You are worth it because you are valued, inherently valued, beautifully valued, and deep down, your soul knows it.

Meditate on these scriptures and then answer the following prompt.

Psalms 139:13-14 (NKJV) For you formed my inward parts: You covered me in my mother's womb. I will praise you, for I am fearfully and wonderfully made: marvelous are your works and that my soul knows very well.

Psalms 139:13-14 (AMP) For you formed my innermost parts; You knit me [together] in my mother's womb. I will give thanks and praise to You, for I am fearfully and wonderfully made; Wonderful are Your works, and my soul knows it very well.

Journal Prompt:

Write about being beautifully valued. How does **Psalms 139:13-14** reinforce your beautiful value?

Chapter 1

Hero

When I was in late elementary school my teacher gave us an assignment where we had to write an essay talking about our hero. I wrote about my dad. I don't remember exactly what I wrote but what I can remember is that I wrote something about how strong he was and how he would do anything for me. What I do remember is that I shared this writing with my dad. I thought he would be ecstatic, proud, even, to see what I had written about him. But I remember my dad, who is a very expressive man anyway, breaking down in tears. It took me by surprise. Had my write-up touched him so much that he was moved to tears? Did my writing have the opposite effect I was going for? Had I hurt his feelings? I was confused but then he turned to me and said, "I know I haven't been these things to you. I'll do better." I didn't want to think that I had upset him so I hugged him and told him it was okay. That's me - always trying to fix things and that's my dad - always honest, even when it hurts. I don't think I quite understood it at this point though. I mean sure he and my mom had been divorced for a little while. At this time, he was remarried, and I didn't see him as much or spend a lot of time with him but I still looked at him with the bright eyes of my younger self. My dad.... the guy who could do anything if he tried, could beat anyone If he wanted, and was smarter than most when he had something to prove, at least in my eyes. From the beginning, my dad was the greatest to me. I was truly a daddy's girl like most little girls who grow up with their father.

I must have been around three or four years old when I can first remember my dad coming to my rescue. I was definitely in preschool. My brother hadn't been born yet or at least I don't remember him being there. My mom, dad, my baby sister, and I lived in an apartment on my beloved West Side of Chicago. I have mostly good memories. Dad practiced bass guitar in the living room while my sister and I danced around. Preschool pictures in big pretty dresses that I refused to take off afterward. Mom would take the walk across the alley to pick me up from school Monday through Friday. Sometimes she would volunteer and spend the day with our class. I remember when our cat gave birth to her kittens. Their soft meows could be heard throughout the apartment and we followed the sound straight to mine and my sister's bedroom closet. I don't remember any trouble in my parent's marriage at this time. But what would a four-year-old know? Anyhow, the only stain on my memories in that apartment would be an unfortunate situation with a friend of my dad's who would stay over sometimes.

It's dark and my sister Is sleeping In the bed across from me. We had two twin-sized beds separated by a little nightstand. My bed was closest to the door. He came into my room like he had done a few times before but the memory is so cloudy now. He sat down on the bed and placed his hand under the cover to touch me in a place where grown men shouldn't touch little girls. It was not the first time he had done it. In fact, I'm sure I was waiting for him to show up. I was awake and alert and waiting. "Ava, you peed on yourself," he whispered as he snatched his hand back. Knowing what I know now it's possible I did it on purpose to stop him from wanting to touch me. (You see, bedwetting is one of the most common regression symptoms of children experiencing sexual abuse - but I digress.) Either on purpose or just a mental defense mechanism, I was happy that it would keep him from touching me. But I was also scared that I would get in trouble for peeing in the bed. My mother happened to also be up late that night to go to the bathroom. She saw him come out of my room and of course, was immediately alarmed. He tried to explain to my mother why he was coming out of her daughter's room in the middle of the night. I think he may have told her something like he was checking on us. I honestly thought her alarm was intended for me. I was more afraid that I was going to get into trouble for peeing in the bed than the fact that my mom had caught a grown man leaving her young daughter's bedroom. Either way, I wanted the heat off me. "He touched me," I told my mom, almost Immediately. Of course, he denied it. I specifically remember him saying I was lying. Questions were asked, allegations were made, allegations were denied, and then the ass-kicking came. My mom told my dad what she had seen. And even though she says he didn't respond quickly enough; I only remember the response being swift and just. Not once was I not believed. My mother believed me. My father believed me. I don't know if it was that night or early that morning but once I told my mom, she promptly told my dad, who promptly put a hurting on that man. All the way down the stairs and out of the front door. I never saw that man again.

That is one of my first memories of my dad, the hero. That is how it's supposed to be. It was my first encounter with what a "loving father" should be. A knight in shining armor, who would protect you and defend your honor. I was safe…always.

Value Gained

I was lucky, no I was blessed that I was believed, the first time. No one doubted me and I'm sure it didn't hurt that he was pretty much caught red-handed. I still didn't tell right away though and that is the case for many. The shame and guilt that comes along with that experience sometimes make it impossible to share with another person. It can keep you Isolated, feeling you're the only one or you're somehow responsible for it all. For so many, I know the story does not end there. For some, abuse, whether it be sexual, physical, or emotional doesn't end after telling someone. For some, it goes on for a long time, and for others it hasn't ended. The trauma of this abuse can kill the innocence inside of you and when no one believes you it kills the innocence you see in others. If this is something that you have experienced or are experiencing, get help. Keep talking until someone believes you. "Be strong and courageous, do not be afraid or tremble in dread before them, for it is the Lord your God who goes with you. He will not fail you or abandon you." **Deuteronomy 31:6 AMP**

I wish my dad had told me that not all men are heroes or knights in shining armor. Sometimes you have to guard yourself because not everyone has your best interest at heart. I wish he would have told me that sometimes even your hero can let you down because no one is perfect. I don't know why bad things happen to us sometimes. I've learned that life doesn't always deal us a fair hand and there is an enemy who means to do you harm. I also know that even if it doesn't feel like it, God sees you and desires for you to be whole. That man was my dad's friend, someone he trusted. He would not have invited that man into our home if he had known that he was even capable of something like that. He could have killed that man. He didn't and couldn't prevent harm from coming my way but he fought for me. The same way my dad fought for me that day is the same way God fights for you every day. He is our hero and our champion even in the darkest of times. He fights for us even when we feel we are losing the battle. He is Elohim Machase Lanu, the God of our refuge, a safe place when everything appears to be crumbling around us. **Psalms 62:8**

Father, help us to remember that you are our protector, it is you who goes before us. You will fight for us and in our weakness, your strength is made perfect. When we feel we are too weak to go on, help us to rest in your strength always. Because when you fight for us, we always win.

Meditate on these scriptures and then answer the following prompt.

Deuteronomy 3:22 (NIV) Do not fear them; the Lord your God himself will fight for you.

Deuteronomy 20:4 (ASV) For Jehovah, your God is he that goeth with you, to fight for you against your enemies, to save you.

Journal Prompts:

Who has been an earthly hero in your life? How does that compare to the scriptures highlighting God, our hero, listed above?

What areas in your life do you need God to fight for you, save you, and be your refuge?

_____
_____
_____
_____
_____
_____
_____
_____
_____
_____
_____
_____
_____
_____
_____
_____
_____
_____
_____
_____

Chapter 2

What's in a name?

When I was born in the wonderful year of our Lord, none of your business, my parents were two youngins' who were just dating but not yet married. My mom was a tender twenty-year-old girl and my dad was just 21. My mom wasn't even old enough to drink let alone have a baby. The most popular girl names in that year were Jennifer and Jessica but I was given the name Ava Lavon Turner - a name which I have come to love but it wasn't always that way. When I was younger, I thought my name was too short - only three letters! Lavon was my mother's middle name and I was okay with that, often combining my first and middle name to make one unique longer name AvaLavon. I would sometimes tell people that it was my full first name but it never quite stuck. I was often known as "little Ava" since I share the name with my aunt, my mom's oldest sister. When I asked my mother how I got my name she would often tell me the story of how after carrying me in her belly for almost nine months when she finally went into labor, she had no idea what she wanted to name me. This was amazing to me because I thought most young girls grow up choosing their children's names. You know, like when we play house or Barbie and you name your kids. By the time I was in elementary school I thought I wanted to have twins so that I could name them Peaches and Orchard or Pepsi and Cola. Horrific, I know. Even now I keep a stash of baby names because you never know. But not my mom - she claims she had no clue and so the story goes: She went into labor and my grandfather (my father's father) took her to the hospital. Her older sister Ava, was there with her through the entire ordeal. As my mom tells it, my birth didn't actually take long at all because I was born an easy-going, and carefree girl. A couple of pushes and I entered the world pretty much pain and fuss-free. It's an ode to my personality today. Like the air sign that I am, I can go with the flow. I'm not going to make a lot of trouble for you. I'm out here...just doing me. When it came time to put a name on the birth certificate my dad still hadn't shown up at the hospital and so my aunt said "Why don't you give her my name? We can give her your middle name." My father's side of the story is a little different. He was working and my mother was well aware of that. He did however make it to the hospital after my delivery. My dad says the name Ava had already been settled on since at the time he and my aunt were very close. They had talked about it and it had already been decided. I would take my aunt's first name and my mom's middle name. Either way, Ava Lavon came to be.

I don't know if my grandmother, the one who originally named my Aunt Ava, thought this much into it but the name Ava may be a version of Eve or Eva, which comes from the Hebrew name Havva meaning "life or lively." The name is also known to mean "birdlike, lively." I mean I guess it could also describe me - light and airy but full of life and energy! At any rate with my first and middle name being settled on, now came the real issue. What would my last name be? Would my mother give me the last name of my father or not? It was decided in that hospital room that I would take the last name of my mother. She was angry with my father for not coming to the hospital, they weren't married and maybe she did not know the state of their relationship or where they were headed. It didn't help that my dad had been warned about signing the birth certificate and the potential threat of child support. After all, they were just a couple of young kids. This makes sense to me and maybe wouldn't have even been a big deal if not for the fact that by the time I was five years old everyone in my family had a different last name from mine. I was born in January and my parents ended up getting married later that same year in October (I guess they figured it out). My mother took my father's last name, Pettis, so then it was just me. My sister was born in March, two years later, and she too would take my father's last name but there was still just me. By October of 1986, my brother was born and he was named after my father as well - first name and all. So...1...2...3...4 Pettis' and me. What's in a name you say? Everything. It matters and I felt so othered by this experience. I was the first born of this family, I was a part of this family, and yet I wasn't. Not when I was the only one with a different last name. When I came of school age it became so blatant that my last name was different from my parents and my siblings. I would ask constantly about changing my last name because I wanted the last name of my sister, my brother, my mother, but most importantly my father. It was our family name. When we went to church, I felt like everyone's last name was Pettis, because my father has all brothers and all of my cousins had that last name. My uncles and my aunts had that last name. My grandparents had that last name. And then there was me…. Ava…. Turner. Just like I had tried to make AvaLavon happen I was going to make Ava Pettis happen. It didn't matter to me what was on my birth certificate or what they called me at school. I was a Pettis. And let me be clear, neither my mother nor my father did anything to make me feel that I didn't belong. They loved me just like they loved my sister and brother. My paternal family also treated me as if Pettis was the name I was born with. At some point, I became known as Ava Pettis everywhere outside of school because people, my extended family mostly, assumed that was my legal last name. Besides the adults in my family, I'm sure that neither my younger siblings nor my cousins even knew that my last name wasn't the same as theirs. But I knew. That's what's In a name.

It has a way of giving you a sense of belonging. It's OUR name. We are a family and that means something. I could never get comfortable around the idea that I was the only one with a different last name. I was different and not in a good way. My young brain thought why wouldn't you want me to have the same name as everyone else in the house? Even when my parents separated and we weren't in the same house I wanted that name. And even when they divorced, I wanted that name. It was my father's name and therefore my birthright. It was the name of the family I loved. There were no other Turners besides myself, my mom (when she finally went back to her maiden name), my aunt for whom I had been named, and her two children. It was their father's name, my maternal grandfather but I didn't really know him. I didn't know that family, I wasn't connected to them in any other way. I wanted the name of MY family. So, in my eyes, I was forgotten, I didn't quite belong. I was pretending to be a Pettis but I wasn't really a Pettis. Not officially...not on paper... where it mattered.

Value Gained

But where it mattered most was in me. I let this idea of it not being official, this feeling of being an outsider seep into other areas of my life. I never felt like I quite fit in with anyone. I've always felt a little awkward, a little on the outside, not all the way in. Having a different name from others in my family was a metaphor for my life. It meant that I didn't quite fit. I was different. My dad told me that it didn't matter what my name was, he was my dad. I wish that he would have continued to tell me that I belonged no matter what.

I had planned to change my name as soon as I turned eighteen and could legally do it on my own, but the older I got, the less it mattered. I secretly thought to myself "I'll be getting married soon anyway. Mostly, the nature of my relationship with my father had changed drastically and it was no longer as important to me if I had his last name or not. On February 25, 1997, when I was fourteen years old, I wrote the following in my diary.

> *"My dad and I are growing so far apart. We are just not as close as we used to be and I know exactly why. Number one, he's just not acting the way a father should act"*

I'm not quite sure what I meant by "the way a father should act" but whatever it was I didn't feel that urgency to belong with him or to him anymore. I felt alone and forgotten by him. I didn't care to have his last name anymore.

Later that same year I wrote:

> *"No matter how hard we try I don't think I will ever really fit into this family. It seems as though we don't belong anywhere."*

This was the same year my mother had her relapse and we had to live with different family members. It contributed to my feelings of being on the outside because I was just a visitor, only passing through. I didn't feel settled. It didn't matter that my family loved me as much as they could. It didn't matter that when our extended family took us in, they did so out of love and never did anything to make us feel like we didn't belong. My child brain just couldn't comprehend what my adult brain now understands. My name didn't mean my family loved me less. A name is important and a name can evolve as you come to the realization of who and whose you truly are.

I read somewhere that most medieval names were more straightforward than the flamboyant introductions given in the television show *Game of Thrones*. It would simply be your father's name, your home village, your occupation, and maybe a notable personal characteristic. I would just be Ava Pettis of Chicago, a social worker and the most chill chick you ever met. But there's something to learn from those extravagant introductions. They would often include things that weren't true…. yet. It was what they aspired to be or what they believed their birthright to be. Almost like the affirmations we use today. Affirmations are statements that are meant to affect your mind on a conscious and a subconscious level. An "I am" statement can inspire you to believe, think, and then act in ways that line up with your morals and goals. It's a declaration of your truth even if it hasn't happened… yet.

The word 'am' is the first-person singular form of "to be" which is to "exist". It is a state of being". It is God who first answered "I AM WHO I AM." And Jesus, His son followed suit. In the book of John alone there are seven "I Am" Statements including "I am the bread of life." **(John 6:35, 41, 48, 51)**. "I am the light of the world." **(John 8:12)** "I am the door of the sheep." **(John 10:7,9)** "I am the resurrection and the life." **(John 11:25)** "I am the good shepherd." **(John 10:11, 14)** "I am the way, the truth, and the life." **(John 14:6)** "I am the true vine." **(John 15:1, 5)**. Am I not also? Should we not follow in the path of God and Jesus and declare "I Am". Truth is, it doesn't matter if my last name is Turner, Pettis, or Blalark, I am known and I am loved by God. I am not 'othered'. I belong. It was a trick of the enemy that I ever felt otherwise. The Turners love me, The Pettis love me, The Blalarks love me. But most importantly regardless of what my last name is, God Loves me. He has called me by my name. I'm reminded of the scripture that says "Everyone who is called by name, whom I have created for My glory; I have formed him, yes, I have made him." **(Isaiah 43:7)**. I am called by HIS name. I fit where I am supposed to fit.

I can fit anywhere I need to fit. He made me, He'll always remember me, I'll never be forgotten. I am Ava Lavon Turner Pettis Blalark and I am everything He says I am and everything I aspire to be.

Isaiah 44:21 is a personal message for me. "I, the Lord, made you (Ava), and I will not forget you (Ava). Always remember, (Ava), you are not forgotten."

Maybe you have a similar story of where you have felt like you didn't belong or you felt othered. Let this be a personal message to you as well, no matter your family of origin or even friends and other groups you may find yourself in, God has called you by name and you belong to him. **Isaiah 43:1** So, boldly declare who and whose you are. I am Ava Turner Blalark Pettis; I am loved by many. I belong to many but most importantly I am a child of and chosen by God.

Meditate on these scriptures and then answer the following prompt.

Roman 8:15 (NKJV) For you did not receive a spirit of bondage again to fear, but you received the Spirit of adoption by whom we cry out, "Abba, Father.

II Corinthians 6:18 (NIV) And, I will be a Father to you, and you will be my sons and daughters, says the Lord Almighty.

Journal Prompts:

Have you ever felt othered or like you didn't belong or that you were forgotten? After meditating on the scriptures, what is God saying to you about belonging?

_____
_____
_____
_____
_____
_____
_____
_____
_____
_____
_____
_____
_____
_____
_____

What will it feel like when you walk into the realization that you are never forgotten?

Write out your full name and follow it with at least five "I AM" statements. Let your statements be the best version of yourself. The person you dream yourself to be. The person God says you are:

_____

_____

_____

_____

_____

_____

_____

_____

_____

_____

_____

_____

_____

_____

_____

_____

_____

_____

_____

Chapter 3

Conflicted

Before God revealed to me that I would always belong, before I walked in the peace that I would never be forgotten, I was indifferent. For a long time, I saw my dad as a hero even when he made choices that showed me otherwise. The image of him coming to my rescue had shaped my young brain so much. I knew what it was supposed to be like. I knew what it could be like because I had experienced it firsthand. Dads were supposed to always be there for you, no matter what. So, when life and choices that my parents would make began to show me that they too were human, I couldn't comprehend it. I didn't want to.

When my mom packed us and our trash bags up and took us to our grandmother's house, I didn't want to go with her. My sister didn't want to go with her. Even though my mother was doing what she should have done - leaving an abusive and toxic relationship I still saw my dad in a different light. I wanted to stay with my father. When we made it to our destination my sister and I cried for days, maybe weeks. We were having fun living with our cousins in that upstairs apartment above our grandmother but seeing dad sporadically was not enough. Our family had been destroyed and, in our eyes, my mother had been the one to do it. I didn't understand that they didn't belong together anymore. I didn't understand that she wasn't physically safe in the house with him anymore. He was still everything to me. I even remember one of my aunts saying to me, "Your mother is doing the best she can." But you cannot reason with a young child. My world had been turned upside down. We must have worn my mother down at some point because my mom packed us up, my dad hopped the bus to come to get us and we went to live with him. It was around 2nd grade. My brother stayed behind with my mother while my sister and I went to live with my dad who was living with and taking care of his grandfather in the house on St. Louis Street. There was a time it was just dad and his girls. I don't remember seeing my mother often but she would come around sometime. My dad did our hair, he cooked our food, and my teachers knew him. I thought it was great! My most important life lesson from my dad was independence. My dad took care of us but he would also be gone a lot, working I always assumed. It was in 2nd grade that he taught us to walk home alone. My teachers did not approve but I remember my dad telling them "Ava is responsible, she can do it." He taught us what to do when we got home. We always had strict rules to keep us safe. Our great grandfather would be home to receive us. If for some reason we had to stay outside or wanted to go out we had to stay inside the fenced gate on the porch until he got home. And somehow, he always knew when we broke the rules and ventured outside the fenced gate even if just for a few minutes. I can't keep track of when things changed but my mom and dad would switch positions in the house on St. Louis Street. I can't count the number of times we went back and forth. I went to two schools in 2nd grade, I lived in the house on St. Louis in 3rd grade and part of 4th grade. Again, in 5th grade and 6th grade. Sometimes we lived there with just my dad. Sometimes, just my mom. Sometimes they both would be there. I still dream of that house. It's the only house we lived in where I was ever able to have my own room. By the end of 6th grade, we were gone from that house for good. If you read *Valued, things I wish my mom would have told me,* then you know the story of how during my 7th grade we would live in a shelter and then back with my grandmother. You know that between 7th and 12th grade there were many places I would call home.

Where was my dad in all of this? I remember when we first went to that shelter. I was hoping that he would save us. I still wanted to be with my father. We were still living in the shelter when on July 10, 1995, I wrote:

> *She [mom] won't let us spend any time with our dad. She shouldn't do that. But I bet if I want to go see him I will, I hope he takes her to court about when he can see us. I hope he wins."*

I wrote that entry with all the spunk and tenacity of a twelve-year-old girl with no real power. At some point, we would stay with my dad again for a short while in the apartment on Jackson street. I remember wearing his jeans in 8th grade because the baggy style was in. They were of course way too big but I rocked them anyway. It was where I introduced my cousins to one of the greatest movies of all time *(The Five Heartbeats)* on VHS of course. It was where I stepped into womanhood and had to get "the talk" from my grandmother.

But, in the years to follow my feelings would begin to change.

> *September 9, 1996*
>
> *"Still haven't heard from my dad. He could at least send a letter or something."*
>
> *August 9, 1997*
>
> *"Tomorrow is my dad's birthday. I am totally pissed with him. And right now, I don't even like him."*

Value Gained

My heart was conflicted and my view was changing. After that short time in 8th grade, I would never live with him again. I already had too many disappointments and I was learning that I couldn't trust him. The image of my hero was a distant memory and the dream was changing. So just like most people who have been hurt or been through any type of trauma our minds get reshaped. Your brain chemistry literally changes in response to trauma. Mentally, you attempt to adapt. In an effort to protect myself from disappointment I tried to force myself to not believe him when he would make promises. Sometimes it worked but most times it didn't. This was the beginning of putting up a wall to protect myself. If I didn't have any expectations, I couldn't be disappointed. If I didn't let you in you couldn't hurt me. People could not be trusted because one minute they would be there and then the next they would not. I could trust myself though, but I too was changing.

Something I learned years later, as an adult when studying trauma, is that my difficulty with a major change in my life was very upsetting due to all of the changes I experienced growing up. While most people on the outside could not see it, I had and still do sometimes have difficulty with change. For me, change rang an alarm in my brain. I needed consistency in a world that had not offered me the courtesy of remaining the same and I tried my best to provide it for myself. You know I love a good quote and at some point, I came across the quote "the only thing constant in the world is change" which was first said by the ancient Greek philosopher Heraclitus but I heard it first from the great songwriter, India Arie. It made so much sense to me, and I tried to live that, I tried to live not crying over spilled milk. Don't expect too much from people because things are always changing. How they feel changes. Houses change, schools change, friends change, parents change. I change. Everything changes. The going back and forth between "he loves me, he loves me not" was too much at times.

But God is consistent. He was there in the beginning and He will be there in the end. He is everlasting and never changing, and that is something I can depend on. No matter what I do, God would never switch up on me. It doesn't matter if I'm good or bad, right or wrong. It doesn't matter if I'm married or single. It doesn't matter if I have a degree or I don't. It doesn't matter if I change. We're always growing as people. I think God knew that. He created us with our own will. We change physically as we grow older. Our mind changes as new information comes to it. In an ever-changing world, our minds strive to make sense of it all and we seek to protect ourselves. We can't change people and sometimes we can't even stop the change that happens within ourselves. But He is not bound by the human constraint that everything changes, that became my solace. In a world of things ever changing I could hold on to God's unchanging hand. There can be growth in change but God is already there. Bigger and greater than it all, He doesn't need to evolve. He is a solid, sturdy, strong, and unchanging foundation.

And we can rest knowing that Jesus Christ is the same yesterday, today, and forever. **Hebrew 13:8 (NKJV).**

Meditate on these scriptures and then answer the following prompt.

Revelation 1:8 (NKJV) I am Alpha and the Omega, the beginning and the End," says the Lord, "who is and who was and who is to come, the Almighty.

Psalms 119:89-89 (NKJV) Forever, O lord, your word is settled in heaven. Your faithfulness endures to all generations: You establish the earth and it abides.

Deuteronomy 7:9 (NKJV) Know therefore that the Lord your God is God; he is the faithful God (El Emunah), keeping his covenant of love to a thousand generations of those who love him and keep his commandments.

Journal Prompts:

In what areas of your life do you feel chaotic and unstable?

_____

_____

_____

_____

_____

_____

_____

_____

_____

_____

_____

_____

_____

_____

_____

_____

Beautifully Valued

How can you trust in the God who keeps his promise of love to a thousand generations? In what ways can you rest in knowing that even in this ever-changing world God is faithful to you. He will keep his covenant of love to you.

Chapter 4

Beauty's only skin deep

They say beauty is in the eye of the beholder. Which I always took to mean that everyone is beautiful to someone. But how about everyone is beautiful...period. It's not just about how you look on the outside but who you are on the inside as well. You can be the most beautiful person on the outside and not even know it because you need to do work on the inside. There is more than one way to be beautiful. My struggle with my self-esteem started with how I looked, physically, comparing myself to others, I sought attention from all the wrong places.

June 28, 1998

"Lately, my sister has been getting all the attention from the opposite sex. I'm kinda losing my self-confidence."

September 13, 1998

"My face has broken out something ugly, and I've lost some of my self-confidence in my appearance. I think I'm getting too desperate for a man. I like any guy I see, and that's bad. But I recognize my problem and I'm going to take care of that. I don't have time for a boyfriend right now. At least that's what I keep telling myself. I'm really depressed about it."

Beautifully Valued

All of my value in physical appearance was coming from how the boys looked at me or didn't look at me. All of my self-confidence was wrapped up in how I looked to others and how boys responded to me. I was in high school truly believing that part of my self-worth was in how the opposite sex perceived me. If boys thought I was cute then I felt good but if they didn't then I didn't feel good. I'm not sure where or how we learn this but I know I'm not the only one who has felt that way and I see it in girls even today. I was too tall, too skinny, my glasses were too thick, and my teeth were too big. All I could focus on was what I considered the negatives. For some people, they are too short, too fat, and their teeth are too small. It took me such a long time to become comfortable in my own skin. And even when I thought I looked pretty on the outside something was still missing. It was what I thought about myself. "Real self-esteem doesn't come from fixing the outside. There is work that needs to be done on the inside. You can improve the outside, but if you don't face your fears, insecurities, and what is going on inside your head, it won't work. What voice do you hear and what is it telling you? Who are you? Is that your idea or someone else's? Sometimes the thoughts in our head become reality even if they are not fact." (*Valued*, 2020)

I read an article, by Biller (1993), that stated that father deprivation can impact female psychosexual development in the following ways:

increased obsession with young males, increased seeking of male attention, idealization of absent fathers, and increased risk of pregnancy. And even though girls may spend more time talking to their mothers about these things, the mere presence of the father promotes healthy self-esteem and psychosexual development.

If the first man I loved could leave, wouldn't they all? If I was not good enough for him, how could I be good enough for another?

Value Gained

I sometimes wish the voice of my father had been louder and affirmed my physical beauty. I wish he had wrapped me up and held me close to tell me that I was beautiful - inside and out. Maybe when I was younger, he did. I knew I felt safe and loved as a five-year-old. But I needed it most as I grew older and went through puberty. I needed it most when my face started to break out and the boys made fun of my big teeth with the gap that my dad is famous for. I don't know if it would have helped but it certainly could not have hurt. What I do remember is my dad often affirming my attributes outside of physical beauty, and even today as a woman what I hear most from him is that I am smart, wise, talented, and gifted. Maybe that is just as important if not more so than physical beauty. When I wrote in *Valued* that you have to find the small quiet voice and strengthen it that voice is the voice of God. I didn't truly walk in knowing my value until I truly began to understand the way God feels about me. My confidence comes from the way that I know He sees me. I am fearfully and wonderfully made; marvelous are Your works! **Psalms 139:14 (NKJV)**. That's me! I am His works and I am marvelous! That's you too! You are His works and You are marvelous!

Young girls ask all the time how they can build their self-esteem or confidence. I've noticed that some girls just have it. They appear confident and exude it, they walk with their head high. Some of us have to work on it and that's okay too. Know your strengths, make a plan for your challenges, and encourage yourself. Sometimes you may even have to fake it until you make it.

I believe in the power of affirmations. Sometimes you really do have to be your own cheerleader and gas yourself up. But there is power in using the word of God to affirm yourself. Beauty is not in the eye of the beholder but beauty is in the eye of the Creator. What He thinks of me is more important than what I think of myself. What He thinks of me is more important than what anyone else thinks of me. What He thinks of me is fact, it is true and it is always good. One of my favorite chapters in the Bible is Romans chapter 8 because there is just so much good stuff there. The entire chapter is one big affirmation of God's love for me and everything I am.

Meditate on these scriptures and then create your own affirmations based on the Word of God.

I am loved.

> **Romans 8:38 (AMP)** For am I convinced [and continue to be convinced - beyond any doubt] that neither death, nor life, nor angel, nor principalities, nor things present and threatening, nor things to come or powers, nor height, nor depth, nor any other created thing, will be able to separate us from the [unlimited' love of God, which is in Christ Jesus our Lord.

I am chosen.

> **Romans 8:30 (AMP)** And those whom He predestined, He also called; and those whom He called, He also justified [declared free of the guilt of sin]; and those whom He justified, He also glorified [raising them to a heavenly dignity].

I have a purpose and good things will happen for me.

> **Romans 8:28 (AMP)** And we know [with great confidence] that God [who is deeply concerned about us] causes all things to work together [as a plan] for good for those who love God, to those who are called according to His plan and purpose.

Beautifully Valued

I am

_____

Scripture(s) that affirm

_____

_____

_____

_____

I am

_____

Scripture(s) that affirm

_____

_____

_____

_____

I am

_____

Scripture(s) that affirm

_____

_____

_____

_____

Chapter 5

The Blues of the Past

The ancient Chinese philosopher Lao Tzu said that depression is living in the past. He specifically said that "If you are depressed, you are living in the past." Modern research suggests that depression can be due to present ongoing difficulties, personal factors, and even brain chemistry but there's some truth to Tzu's quote. When you're stuck thinking about the way things used to be or something difficult that has happened it can be hard to move on, especially if you think it will never get better. Maybe you're stuck on an experience or experiences so awful that you cannot move forward. Oftentimes we think, "what did I do to deserve that or what could I have done differently or why did they do that to me?"

I was stuck. In my mind, everything had been perfect before my parents had ruined it. Not only had they ruined it but they weren't doing anything to make it better. I was stuck and it was hard to move on. It's especially difficult when you're a child and you feel that you don't have much control anyway. The truth is it was never quite that simple but when you're a child you make sense of things the only way you know how.

Nov. 9, 1997

It's all my parent's fault. It's because of them I'm never happy. I never

> *get to keep my things because we're always moving and things are always getting left behind."*

I am quite sure I was depressed. I was sad more days than not. I was feeling worthless, I wasn't able to concentrate at school some days, and I was tired and drained both physically and mentally. That, my friends, is the simple definition of clinical depression. But because mental health or just mental well-being overall was never a topic brought up in my household or any of my friends' households it was another thing that made me feel othered. I was different in my feelings from everyone else and something was wrong with me because I couldn't just pray it away. The truth is, knowing what I know now, I'm sure I wasn't alone. I'm sure there was someone else who felt the same but we were all silenced in shame or pride or both. Today I believe we are making progress and becoming more comfortable with topics concerning our mental health.

One in 5 US adults experience mental illness and 17% of young people ages 6-17 experience mental health issues (www.nami.org) so looking back on it now, I know I couldn't have been the only one but it felt like I was. Looking back on it now, I know my father must have dealt with his own issues. Being incarcerated and away from your family. The drugs, the alcohol, etc. I saw him cry a lot. I always thought that he was just emotional, maybe he was overwhelmed too.

August 30, 1996:

"Life is so messed up. There is too much pressure on me. I'm only 14, aren't I supposed to be enjoying life?"

March 13, 1997:

"Man, this week has been tough. Too much stress for a 15-year-old. But maybe, just maybe it will all work out for the best. Never expect too much."

July 16, 1997:

"I'm so unhappy. I don't know why. Sometimes I'm happy, sometimes I'm not. [It's] difficult to understand."

We know that childhood trauma like the loss of a parent contributes to both physical and mental health ailments in adulthood. Amato (1991) found that any form of father loss, including father absence, is associated with depression in adulthood. This was found to be especially true for African-American women.

Value Gained

As a child, it was an ongoing present stressor but as an adult these experiences became past. I knew I wanted to get through it but how? I am not alone, I have never been alone, and I will never be alone. I don't know if my dad dealt with mental illness. I know that he experienced a lot. I can't imagine the mental toll that being incarcerated took on him but It's not something that we've ever talked about.

The hopelessness that comes with depression is due in part to the feeling that things suck now and they will suck forever. I am grateful that was one thing that has always been a relative strength for me. Even though I dealt with the sadness in my mind and I blamed my parents and I didn't know if it would get better, I had a little bit of hope. I had always planned to be better than my parents, to create a life for myself that was better, and if I ever had children, a better life for them.

> *December 14, 1997*
>
> *"I promise myself (and you are my witness) my children will have better. Everything that they want and need. They'll never have to worry about losing me or where they want to live. I used to want to be like my dad. That's when I thought he was the greatest."*

Matthew 7:11 (AMP) If you then, evil (sinful by nature) as you are, know how to give good and advantageous gifts to your children, how much more will your Father who is in heaven [perfect as He is] give what is good and advantageous to those who keep on asking Him. My heavenly father is the greatest. He will give me the things I want and need. He will give me good and advantageous gifts because He is perfect, and I want to be like Him.

My dad never came across as a stereotypical addict. He still always seemed like he had it together even though he did not. I didn't understand it then but that is one thing I admired (and still do) about him most and I think he knew something then that I have only just begun to grasp. He appeared confident more often than not, and his attitude was always one of "I'll figure it out or it's not that bad." In order to get unstuck from living in the past and move forward, you have to live in the present moment and believe that things will be better, that there is a light at the end of the tunnel. Live in the present moment. Live in God's truth. The turning point for me has been focusing on God's love for me. Because he loves me so much and because I believe that it's true, I have hope that everything He promised will be true for me. I believe that he has loved me with an everlasting love and that he replenishes my sorrowful soul **(Jeremiah 31:3, 25 NKJV).** I believe that His joy is my strength (**Nehemiah 8:10 NKJV).** I also believe that when I just feel too weak to go on that His strength is made perfect in my weakness (**II Corinthian 12:9 NKJV).** I don't need to be strong on my own. I don't have to feel ashamed or othered when I'm not quite feeling myself because I know that I am still Ava. I don't need to be perfect; things don't have to be perfect. All I need to focus on is the Word of God and His truth. Sometimes I need a quick check-in with my therapist and I thank God that He's given knowledge to doctors, scientists, therapists, engineers, etc. so that we can have healing in EVERY area of our life. And when I can't pull my thoughts together still, I let go and just free fall because the thoughts that HE thinks towards me are thoughts of peace, to give me a future and hope. **(Jeremiah 29:11 NKJV)**

Meditate on these scriptures and then answer the following prompt.

Romans 8:18 (AMP) For I consider (from the standpoint of faith) that the suffering of the present life is not worthy to be compared with the glory that is about to be revealed to us and in us!

Ephesians 2:10 (NKJV) For we are his workmanship, created in Christ Jesus for good works, which God prepared beforehand, that we should walk in them."

Journal Prompt:

What is an area of your life where you feel stuck or that you have lost hope? What does the Word of God say concerning this area so that you can begin to renew your mind?

_____

_____

_____

_____

_____

_____

_____

_____

_____

_____

_____

_____

_____

Chapter 6

Into the Unknown

If you are depressed you are living in the past but if you are anxious you are living in fear of the future. It's the uncertainty of tomorrow for you and I know this struggle all too well. When you don't know where you will live next or what school you might attend next or if your parent will come home that night, you have perfected living in the unknown. Will I be able to go with my friends to a certain place, will my school fee be paid, will I be able to join an activity if it costs? You're always hyper-aroused and on edge but never fully prepared because how could you be? Young girls need at least low levels of support from their paternal figures to have this support positively impact their level of hope for the future (Denise Davis-May 2004). Hope reflects a person's belief in their ability to achieve certain goals, thus affecting academic achievement, healthy emotional development, and successful transition to adulthood.

On November 9, 1997, when I wrote *"we're always moving and things are always getting left behind"* it was probably around the same time I decided there's no use crying over spilled milk, but remember what else I said about 'spilled milk" - even if you cleaned it up really good it still happened. The milk was still spilled. Anxiety is what you get when you always anticipate more milk spilling and not being able to clean It up in time before even more spills.

> *June 11, 1997*
>
> *"Now that my dad is back in my life I wonder if he's here for good or just passing through."*
>
> *June 17, 1997*
>
> *"He said he was coming over to give me the money but he didn't. He didn't return my call after he promised he'd be there."*

I was on the edge. And just like I teach my clients, being on edge or in constant defense mode is a mechanism our brain uses in order to protect us. If I can anticipate the problem, maybe I can prevent the harm it will cause. The problem occurs when that alarm system in the brain is constantly triggered even when there is no harm present. Sometimes the harm is emotional and not actual, physical danger but our response is all the same. That constant alarm ringing makes it difficult when you're trying to regulate yourself and can't seem to do so. It will take a toll on your body mentally and physically.

> *December 14, 1997*
>
> *"My nerves are starting to get to me. I'm scratching sores on my body again."*

This is only a very recent revelation made about myself. As I read this journal entry my immediate thought was "Oh my God...did I engage in self-harm? Is this how I coped?!" Whenever I think back on the days as a child when my legs would be covered in sores from scratching, I always assumed it was because of my eczema but reading this revealed something new for me. I wasn't scratching because I itched all the time. Sometimes I was scratching because I was overwhelmed. "My nerves" as I called it were getting to me. I was on high alert. Right before this sentence, I wrote about being angry with my parents and blaming them for everything I thought was wrong in my life. I was trying to control the uncontrollable in my life. I think the scratching came from anger, fear, and worry (and maybe eczema too). I couldn't stop because I didn't know how to cope with what I was feeling. I did not tell anyone because I didn't even know what was happening.

I did not know who could be trusted. I wasn't sure that someone was going to show up for me. So how do you deal with that? You try to cope the best way you can. I wrote and I scratched apparently. I learned that I was one of the few people I could rely on. But in the real world, you do have to rely on others sometimes and in the real world, something could happen that makes it difficult for you to carry out what you trusted even yourself to do.

Value Gained

The thing that I've realized about anxiety is it's not only fear of the unknown. It's not just not knowing what's going to happen or what people will think but it's the fear that you won't be able to handle what's happening when it happens. This world isn't perfect, no one is immune to life, and as the saying goes "sh*t happens." What has been the most helpful for me is knowing that even though life isn't perfect I *will* be able to deal with whatever comes my way even if it's really bad. I don't have to be perfect either and it will still be okay. God's Word tells us over and over again that even in the middle of difficult times He is there. He is trustworthy, and He is consistent. It will work out. So, you can count it all joy when you fall into various trials, knowing that the testing of your faith produces patience **(James 1:2-3).** Remind yourself that the sufferings of this present time are not worthy to be compared with the glory which shall be revealed in us **(Romans 8:18)**. *And* I know that in the world I will have tribulation; but I can be of good cheer because God has overcome the world **(John 16:33).**

I have hope, true hope, real hope that it will be okay. That's what faith is...it is made up of the things you hoped for, the things you have waited for. It is your evidence of the things to come - Hebrews 11:1. You didn't do anything to deserve this, and you still deserve the best. You are still beautifully valued. You can choose how you react and and also choose your weapon of choice when the unexpected comes your way. I choose to fight with relaxation techniques, mindfulness strategies, and grounding exercises. I focus on my breathing and my thoughts when I feel I'm spiraling. And even then, I don't always get it right. But my greatest weapon is the Word of God.

December 14, 1997

"I promise myself (and you are my witness) my children will have better. Everything that they want and need. They'll never have to worry about losing me or where they want to live. I used to want to be like my dad. That's when I thought he was the greatest."

Even in my pain, there was a sliver of hope for the future. That when I became an adult, I would be a different parent - one that my children could always depend on. In this, I found that I always have a loving parent that I can always depend on. Because if I, being a regular person, wanted to give good gifts to my children, how much more would my Father who is in heaven give good things to me when I ask Him **Matthew 7:11 (NKJV).** Yes, God wants you to experience all of the good things too. And we can walk in things knowing that God has prepared us for them beforehand.

Meditate on these scriptures and then answer the following prompt.

Philippians 4:6-7 (AMP) Do not be anxious or worried about anything, but in everything [every circumstance and situation] by prayer and petition, with thanksgiving, continue to make your [specific] requests known to God. **7:** and the peace of God [that peace which reassures the heart, that peace] which transcends all understanding, [that peace which] stands guard over your hearts and your minds through Christ Jesus [is yours].

Philippians 4:8 (NKJV) Finally brethren, whatever things are true, whatever things are noble, whatever things are just, whatever things are pure, whatever things are lovely, whatever things are of good report if there is any virtue and if there is any praise - meditate on these things.

Journal Prompts:

In what areas of your life have you struggled with fear of the unknown?

How have you let your thoughts consume your thinking and allow anxiety or worry to creep in? What is God saying to you regarding the peace he desires you to have?

_____
_____
_____
_____
_____
_____
_____
_____
_____
_____
_____
_____
_____
_____
_____
_____
_____

Write down a list of your most worrisome thoughts. Talk to God about them. What is He saying to you in regards to this specific thought?

Chapter 7
Rejection

In writing this I realized that the father-daughter relationship is something quite different from the mother-daughter relationship. Coley (1998) emphasizes the importance of a father-daughter relationship, stating that girls are more positively impacted by relationships with their fathers than boys. As important as the mother-daughter relationship is, God intended something special for the father-daughter relationship, and when it is missing it can have a long-lasting impact. How else do we explain the fact that involvement from a father can positively or negatively affect a woman's academic, behavioral and social, and psycho-social development in such a profound way? That longing, that wanting for a father or father figure is so crucial because it can impact so many areas of our life. It's as if we unconsciously know it so our souls long for it, searching for it.

All I ever wanted was him. I wanted him to be the dad I remembered coming to my rescue when the boogeyman made an appearance at night. I wanted him to show up when he said he was coming. I wanted him to pick me up and to do the things that he had promised he would do, and when it became clear to me that wasn't going to happen something inside of me changed. I shut it down…all the way down. The feeling of disappointment and feeling rejected became overwhelming. Is it me? No, it's not me, it's him. So, stop letting him do this to you. Fool me once, shame on you but shame on me if I continue to allow it to happen. Don't believe what he says, always have a plan B. That way if he comes through, you'll be pleasantly surprised but at least you won't be disappointed. How else does a young girl make sense out of rejection from the one man who is supposed to love her? It is our body's way of protecting us after so many letdowns.

What is the root of your fear of rejection: When was the first time you felt rejected? It can show up as one of two extremes when one feels neglected or dismissed by the very person or people who are supposed to accept all of you and guide you. Maybe you become what I like to think of as 'fiercely independent'. I don't need anyone or anything, I can do this by myself and on my own. You don't let anyone in because you fear they may reject you. Extreme independence isn't the badge of honor I once thought it was. This fear of rejection enables you to push others away. It's a response to trauma and it is exhausting. On the opposite end of the spectrum, maybe you're extremely needy. You neglect the process of coming into the fullness of who you are because you're wrapped up in what others expect you to be. You need acceptance so that you don't feel alone because you feel like you can't do it alone. You look to anyone for the approval you so desperately need. Your need for acceptance is also fear that they may reject you, so you do everything in your power to hold on even when it's bad for you. It's a response to trauma and it too is exhausting.

It's draining to constantly think: I'm not worthy of others' help so I try to do it all myself. It's also crushing to constantly think: I'm not enough for others so I try to be everything for others. Both thoughts are rooted in fear, fear of rejection, fear of disappointment, just fear.

Value Gained

But God did not give us a spirit of fear but of love, power, and a sound mind **(2 Timothy 1:7 NKJV)**. In fact, the amplified version calls "sound mind", sound judgment, and personal discipline [abilities that result in a calm, well-balanced mind and self-control]. God will heal you of your fear of rejection and give you sound judgment and personal discipline to know who is worthy of your love and your affection. And when you make mistakes, as we all do, He will help you to heal and give you peace in the situation. You will learn and you will grow. He has given you the ability to become self-aware to learn and identify your emotions and to know your triggers. He has given you the ability to find balance and not to let your emotions overtake you. The areas in your life that seem dead due to fear and rejection can come alive again because of God, who gives life to the dead and calls those things which do not exist as though they did; **(Romans 4:17 NKJV).**

Meditate on these scriptures and then answer the following prompt.

Romans 8:15 (NKJV) For you did not receive the spirit of bondage again to fear, but you received the Spirit of adoption by whom we cry out, "Abba, Father."

II Corinthians 9:8 (NKJV) And God is able to make all grace abound toward you, that you, always having all sufficiency in all things, may have an abundance for every good work."

Journal Prompts:

Have you faced rejection at any point in your life? If so, in what ways did you handle it?

_____
_____
_____
_____
_____
_____
_____
_____
_____
_____
_____
_____
_____
_____
_____
_____
_____

How can the words of the Father help you to know that you do not have to fear being more than enough and worthy of love, happiness, and beautiful relationships?

_____
_____
_____
_____
_____
_____
_____
_____
_____
_____
_____
_____
_____
_____
_____
_____
_____
_____

Chapter 8
The choice: Loving the one who hurt you

That feeling of fear and rejection was real and by the time middle school came around, I was indifferent. I was guarded. The man who I first knew as my hero wasn't living up to that. He hadn't kept his promise to "do better". If he could do anything, why wasn't he doing something? Why wasn't he coming to my rescue like he had when I was 4 years old? How could my hero become the antagonist in my story?

Like my mother, my dad had his own demons to fight which kept him from fulfilling the promise to do better for me.

September 15, 1996 "My dad's out of jail!" I wrote that sentence with excitement and hope but less than 6 months later……

> *February 27, 1997 "I hate my dad for what he has become. It is with tears I write this because I really do love him…. Why doesn't he care anymore?"*
>
> *June 11, 1997 "I used to want to be like my dad." That's when I thought he was the greatest."*

The inner conflict I endured during this time was enormous. I love him, I hate him. He loves me, he loves me not. At some point, I thought well enough of him to write that he was my hero for a school assignment. The one who fixed me and my sister's hair, the awesome artist, the guy who I thought could beat anyone. At some point, none of that mattered because he wasn't "the greatest" anymore. He had fallen short. One of the most important relationships a girl can have is the one she has with her father. He shows her how a man should treat her. He shows her how a man should love her, and the effects can be detrimental if dad isn't around. You've heard of 'daddy issues'. It's been said she may seek to find love and attention from men in order to fill that void. A child's relationship or, lack of, with their father can even affect their educational success, especially for African American girls. The pregnancy rates, prison rates, and suicide rates are much higher for children who live in fatherless homes. And sometimes, even when there is a loving father in the home, we make decisions that lead us down these paths. My dad had a great dad and he was a great grandfather. My father shared with me that my grandfather looked at my dad the same way I did, with the expectation that he could do anything. That only changed when my father began to deal drugs. My father remembers my grandfather saying "I have pity for the drug user but I have none for the dealer." And he was ashamed. I could hear the pain in my dad's voice even now, when he told me "I broke his heart."

Value Gained

But my grandfather still loved my father. My grandparents were the grace of God because they took care of my father and his family when my father was unable to. This is what I mean by not using unforgiveness as an excuse or letting it hold you back from your greatness. Just like my grandfather had forgiven my dad, I choose to forgive my dad. My grandfather did not let my father's mistakes stop him from loving him. And try as I might I could not stop loving my dad either. Just like he never stopped loving me or my siblings. I recognized early on that my dad had demons he was dealing with that would prevent him from being a present father in our lives. But I promised myself I would not be another statistic. I could have engaged in behavior and activity that got me in trouble. I could have taken my anger and my sadness out on the world but I knew that was not the life I wanted for myself so I had to be very careful. I had to be careful about the friends I chose, and the places I went to, and make the decisions that would get me where I wanted to go.

Lower educational success wasn't my story. I didn't become a teenage mother; I didn't go to prison and I'm still alive. This is my story, I write the narrative, and I decide the ending even when there's a detour.

Love is a choice. My grandparents chose to continue to love their son even when he had hurt them deeply. They continued to hope and never gave up on him. I choose to love my dad, and he chooses to love me. He could hide in shame, overcome by the guilt of his past but he chooses love. God chooses to love us in spite of all that we do. He chooses hope and desires that we all come to him and choose Him as well. I choose love because the alternative is hate. Pain is inevitable but suffering is a choice. Healing is a personal responsibility; you can choose it as well. If you are at peace you are living in the present. What matters most is the person you are now and the way you choose to live your life from today forward.

In 2013 my dad wrote a letter to his children. Each of us got a separate letter in the mail. We've never shared what was in our letters because the words are personal for each of us, I'm sure. In my letter, my dad stated that he realized he didn't know me very well anymore but that he wanted to build a relationship. He wanted to say he was sorry. He wanted me to know that while he couldn't do anything about the past, he was choosing a better future. The letter came as somewhat of a surprise to me because while it wasn't perfect our relationship was already well on its way to healing for me. But, I believed, that was part of his personal healing journey.

Just like I did not need an apology from my mom, I did not need an apology from my dad because just like my mother I had already chosen to forgive him. Like my mother, I believe the apology helped him because it allowed them to forgive themselves.

My dad is a present figure in my life. He checks in on me and my family and I know that if I needed him for anything he would answer. He's finally keeping his promise. But before we got to that point there was healing that was needed. Before he was able to be present in my life, I had to learn to rely on the Heavenly Father to be my hero and to remind me of how beautifully valued I really was. To know that he wanted me to prosper in *EVERY* area of my life. "Beloved, I pray that in every way you may succeed and prosper and be in good health [physically], just as [I know] your soul prospers [spiritually]. **3 John 1:2 (AMP)**

Meditate on these scriptures and then answer the following prompt.

Jeremiah 3:3 (NKJV) The Lord has appeared of old to me, saying: Yes, I have loved you with an everlasting love; therefore, with lovingkindness, I have drawn you.

Jeremiah 1:5 (NKJV) Before I formed you in the womb I knew you; before you were born I sanctified you; I ordained you a prophet to the nations.

Beautifully Valued

Ephesians 2:10 For we are His workmanship, created in Christ Jesus for good works, which God prepared beforehand that we should walk in them them.

Journal Prompts:

Think about the goals you have for your life. What have you let stop you from going after your goals?

_____
_____
_____
_____
_____
_____
_____
_____
_____
_____
_____
_____
_____
_____
_____

What areas in your love are in need of healing? How can you choose your healing and choose love in your life today?

Chapter 9

Father Figures - Gratitude

That constant longing for a father figure can lead you to some dangerous places. It can leave a void that only a father can fill but if you think you've found it in other men, food, drugs, or social media, you may find yourself continuing to long. It's so easy to focus on the negative things. It's easy to focus on what we lack so that we may actually miss what we do have. I once read that one of the evils of the human psyche is to remember the bad. While it can be daunting, I also think that sometimes we remember the bad out of necessity. As I've said, focusing on the negative helps us to protect ourselves from future hurt. It's a leftover biological mechanism. For example, if you get bitten by a dog or have a negative experience with a dog when you're younger you're less likely to socialize with the animal in the future. But if you grew up with dogs and have had nothing but positive experiences with them, you're likely to try to pet most dogs you see. Our experiences shape us. But we cannot let them prevent us from seeing the good around us or missing out on beautiful relationships. So, we have to remember the good just as much if not more so. The antidote to our forgetfulness is an intentional memory of gratitude. "Let all that I am praise the Lord; may I never forget the good things he does for me" **(Psalms 103:2 NLT).**

Expressing gratitude to God, to others, and to yourself creates happiness and other positive emotions. It helps to improve relationships, and mental and physical health. When we look for the positive, we change our brain chemistry. There is an entire psychology around positive thinking that is supported by neuroscience and research. It literally changes your brain chemistry. The part of your **brain responsible for** regulating emotions, memory, and bodily functioning, gets activated with feelings of gratitude. There have been clinical studies that show that people who keep a gratitude journal experience fewer pain symptom (Emmons & McCullough, 2003). It can reduce anxiety and depression and improve sleep quality. It's amazing what gratitude can do.

What I find even more amazing is that the Heavenly Father already knew what gratitude was able to do for us. Gratitude is the act of being thankful, ready to show appreciation for, and to return kindness. It is given and received. It is expressive and receptive because when you give, you get something back. You get peace, you get joy, and most importantly you receive enough. This is why the scripture says to rejoice in the Lord always. Again, I will say, rejoice! **(Philippians 4:4)** To rejoice always in **1 Thessalonians 5:16** and to give thanks in everything just 2 verses down in **Thessalonians 5:18.** For this is the will of God in Christ Jesus for you. It is His will that you give thanks in everything so that your brain chemistry can be rewired. Gratitude is a natural remedy to life's problems. I believe God created us with a need to achieve the delicate balance between remembering true danger to protect yourself and intentional focus on gratitude so that you are not overcome or overwhelmed with the former.

I recently listened to a neighbor talk about the loss of his father "...there's a hole in me, there's something missing. We did everything together." I was overcome with empathy for him. What an awesome relationship they must have had that they did everything together. How sad he must feel now that his father is gone. And also, what a testimony to be able to feel that way about someone. How wonderful to have such beautiful memories. If you're a *This Is Us* fan like me it brings to memory the line that says something like "...if you miss something or it makes you sad when it's gone it must have been pretty wonderful while it was happening."

If your earthly father was present in your life what a gift God has given you to know such an earthly love. And if you are longing for an earthly father, what a gift God has given you to know the love of the Father. A love that knows no boundaries, a love that covers all, that never fails and never gives up on you. They are both true for you. He will keep you in perfect peace **(Isiah 26:3).** The word peace or shalom is literally translated to mean completeness, soundness, quiet contentment, tranquility, friendship, and relationship with humans and God. Nothing is missing, nothing is broken. You lack or want for nothing.

It ain't always easy but I choose gratitude.

My grandfather, just like I spoke of my grandmother before, was an awesome earthly example for me. A man who came to my rescue spiritually, financially, and emotionally even though he wasn't a very emotional guy. I'm thankful for discipline when I needed it. I am grateful for never having to go hungry and for my love of strawberry-filled birthday cake.

I am grateful for my uncle who took us in while supporting 5 children of his own. I am thankful for his honesty and his selfless giving.

What an inspiration to see my father-in-law with his daughters and to be able to call him dad as well.

What an honor and a privilege to watch my son and his father. To know that my child and future children will know such love.

What a blessing to have memories of riding my bike in the park and dance parties in the living room while dad played bass guitar. He's where I get my smarts from, my love of music, and my "can do anything" attitude.

Meditate on these scriptures and then answer the following prompt.

Romans 5:3 (ASV) ...we also rejoice in our tribulations: knowing that tribulation worketh steadfastness.

2 Cor. 10:5 - casting down arguments and every high thing that exalts itself against the knowledge of God, bringing every thought into captivity to the obedience of Christ.

Journal Prompts:

What "arguments" or thoughts are coming against the knowledge of God that you are loved and how can you bring them into captivity?

Who is one person or one thing that you are grateful for and why?

Conclusion

Restoration

One of my first thoughts when writing this was "wow I was really angry." And it made me sad how angry I was with my father. It was an emotional journey and I started to question am I really healed from this like I say that I am? Should I even be writing this book? And the answer was and is yes. Even when my confidence would begin to waver and I would need to walk away from this writing I always came back knowing that it needed to be done. This is part of the process. Being able to express emotions freely without guilt or shame is part of the healing. Emotions are powerful and useful but temporary if we allow them to be.

In Psalms 23 David writes "He restoreth my soul...." The word restoreth means to return or to turn back, to bring back...restore, refresh, and repair. And while God can do anything in an instant He is not bound by our human concept of time. In our limited human understanding and sometimes unwise choices, this healing and restoring often takes time and is a process, steps taken to achieve a particular end. In those moments when I feel as though I can't trust anyone or anything I know that I can trust and have confidence in God. If I don't lean to my understanding (because it often doesn't make sense in our minds), if I rely on the wisdom of God, he will direct my path - in life, in business, in school, in my relationships, and my decision making **(Proverbs 3:5-7).** My best friend likened it to that of a baby who fully trusts in their momma. Most of the time, I just close my eyes and leap, knowing He will catch me.

And when I question my beautiful value, He sends me a reminder of just how dope I am in the form of a text or a message from a friend and sometimes a stranger. The reminders come from my dad when he tells me I got "all of the good stuff and none of the bad." Sometimes it's just the still small voice of how awesome He made me and how He made me with a specific purpose in mind.

The same way I know that I had a special place in my grandmother's heart and I know I have a special place in my dad's heart is the same way I know that I have a special place in God's heart. I am His favorite. I am his beloved child. I did not receive the spirit of bondage again to fear, but I received the Spirit of adoption by whom I cry out, "Abba, Father. The spirit Himself bears witness with my spirit that I am a child of God, and if a child, then an heir - heir of God and a joint heir with Christ, if indeed I suffer with Him, that I may also be glorified together" **Romans 8:15-17 (NKJV).**

It is personal for me. All of His promises for me are Yes and Amen! I know that all of the "things" work together for my good **(Romans 8:28).**

I couldn't see it then but I see it now. What a testimony. I bet you have one too.

> *December 1, 2006*
>
> *"Oh, my goodness! I'm almost 25 and I still occasionally write in my diary. Quick fill in: I graduated, twice! I live alone. I'm pretty independent. I've come a long way since 1995. Looking back on all that stuff it's just amazing. God has brought me so far."*

And He will continue to do so.

References:

The Bible

Amato, P.R. (1994). Father-child relations, mother-child relations, and offspring psychological well-being in early adulthood. Journal of Marriage and the Family, 56(4), 1031-1042.

Bowlby, J. (1988). A secure base: parent-child attachment and healthy human development. New York: Basic Books, Inc.

Coley, R.L. (1998). Children's socialization experiences and functioning in single-mother households: The importance of fathers and other men. Child Development, 69(1), 219-230.

Denise Davis Maye (2004) Daddy's little girl, Journal of Children and Poverty, 10:1, 53-68, DOI: 10.1080/1079612042000199232

The Neuroscience of Gratitude and How it Affects anxiety & Grief by Madhuleena Roy Chowdhury, BA

www.ingramcontent.com/pod-product-compliance
Lightning Source LLC
Chambersburg PA
CBHW070323120526
44590CB00017B/2797